OPEN
HEART
UNIVERSITY

I am the pen,
  without me this paper
cannot live.

OPEN HEART UNIVERSITY

POEMS

Spike Milligan

illustrations by
Laura Milligan and Jack Hobbs and
Spike Milligan

M & J HOBBS
in association with
MICHAEL JOSEPH

First published in Great Britain by M. and J. Hobbs,
25 Bridge Street, Walton-on-Thames,
Surrey and Michael Joseph Ltd,
52 Bedford Square, London WC1
1979

ISBN 0 7181 1757 3

Printed in Great Britain by
Hollen Street Press, Slough and
bound by Dorstel Press, Harlow

This book is dedicated
to S.S. who gave me
heaven and hell

July 1978

Omen of emptiness

The clock has turned enough
        to reach a planet

Life is endless night
I hear wings beating in
        the dark of my room

A giant Raven is waiting —
        for me to fall asleep

Winter 1977

6

When I Suspected

There will be a time when it will end.
Be it parting
Be it death
So each passing minute with you
                       pendulumned with sadness.
So many times
I looked long into your face.
                I could hear the clock ticking.

On a plane over Java
November 1977

Laura Mishgan

Unfaithful She

Dedicated to S.S.

The sight of you
      rent the heaven in two
The gasp in your voice
      could do that too
That the sky would fall
      with a telephone call
And leave me standing in an empty hall.
So folly runs like wine
      but the empty glass is mine.
You leave no choice
      save the lasting taste of brine

Envoi

It was you,
      that poisoned the morning dew

Bayswater
November 1977

A Present for the Future

To Miss J.G.

Green earrings I bought her
           from Maori Shores.
When I returned,
           she had gone
and taken her ears with her.

Earrings made from Pacific Jade—
           you could see through them
Why didn't I see through her?

A-Have-It-Away-Day

To Miss J.G.

I asked a friend how I lost her.
'She met a man on a train
                    and fell in love with him.'
Money is not all the British Railways are
                                      losing.

True Love, Until

Dedicated to S.S.

In bed she said 'I love you'
She said it to my face.
I remember as each silver word
Fell carefully in place.

Continental Envoi

In bed she said 'I love you'
To many another face.
And once again each silver word
Fell carefully in place.

January 1978

Feelings

There *must* be a wound!
No one can be this hurt
         and not bleed.

How could she injure me so?
      No marks
      No bruise

Worse!
People say 'My, you're looking well'
. . . . . . God help me!
      She's mummified me—
          ALIVE!

Bayswater
December 1977

Feelings.

There **must** be a wound!
No one can be this hurt
      and not bleed.

How could she injure me so?
      No marks
      No bruise

Worse!
People say 'My, your looking well'
..... God help me!
    Shes mummified me —
          ALIVE!

Dec 77
Bayswalk

Welcome Home

Unaware of my crime
        they stood me in the dock.

I was sentenced to life . . . .
                without her.

Strange trial.
      No Judge.
      No Jury.

I wonder who my visitors will be.

Bayswater
December 1977

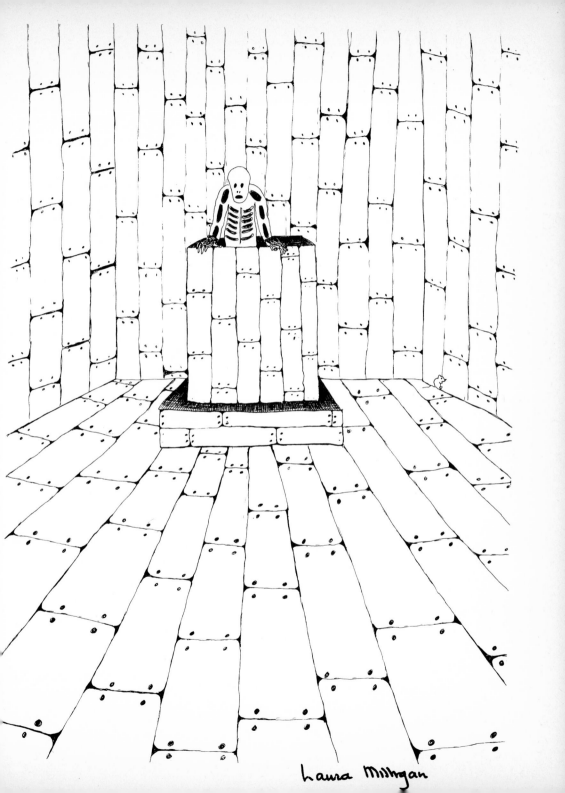

Laura Milligan

Revenge

To Miss J.G.

She once made beautiful Easter Eggs.
Down the years
        the clumsy broke theirs.
I kept mine safe.
Today, I broke it.
I used a dove's feather.
I'm not a vicious person.

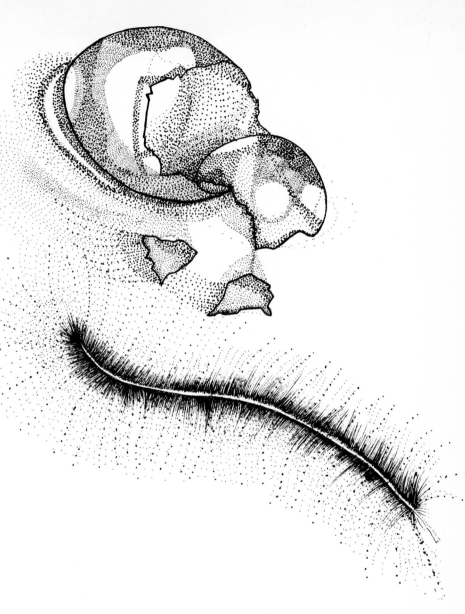

Laura Milligan

Goodbye S.S.

Go away girl, go away
    and let me pack my dreams
now where did I put those yesteryears
    made up with broken seams
Where shall I sweep the pieces
    my God they still look new
Theres a taxi waiting at the door
    but theres only room for you

Food of Love.

Four years she ate my dinners
Four years she drank my wines
And all the while.
I was nourishing her
For some other crummy swines.

Bayswater
1477

Finale

The Queen stumbles
        the bones of heaven
        torque in winds of death.

Black Swan
        course the Styx.
Warriors burn your shields,
        sand the blood-folded fields.

Turrets catch the King's grief
        White handed he paces the air
        with mindless fingers.

Fires sorrow the night
        in dead-finery she biers
Wax-ready for unknown journeys

Pass on black-blench waters. . . . .

Laura Milligan

The Light That Failed

To Shelagh

It's this darkness at noon—
I can hear the boat sailing
I thought I knew where the switch was
Everything was so bright,
The picture was nearly finished
Even the eyes seemed perfect
So what happened to the light?
It must have been an eclipse. . . . .
Mine. . . . .

1977

Laura Mishgan

Euro love

I cannot
   and I will not
   no, I cannot love you less
Like the flower to the butterfly
The corsage to the dress

She turns my love to dust
      my destination empty
         my beliefs scattered: Diaspora!

Who set this course. - and why?
Now my wings beat -
            without purpose
Yet they speed.............

Dedicated to S.S.

26

Laura Milligan

My Daughter of 5 – Jane

The midnight clock
    cuts hours into the dark

 That picture of you
    stilled by sleep
    one dream ahead
    as children always are.

Little Jane
    you colour my tired mind
Opening gates in long forgotten
        child meadows
Where once I ran through summer grasses
    now, it grows for you.

Finchley
4 December 1969
1.40am

Laura Milligan

Easter 1916

The lights had gone out!
    The sun cannot set!
    The green heart is suppurating!
Heroes' souls are on the English rack
    and the harp's strings are muted.

In the fusillade
    a child is born in blood,
    his heritage will be glory.

Goodnight Padraic Pearse
    and your friends.

February 1975

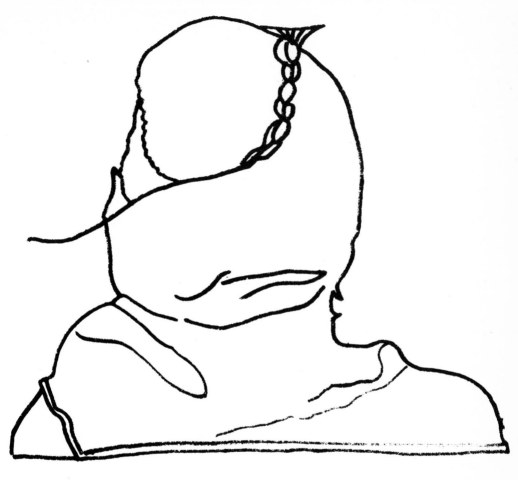

Spike Milligan

That we should meet
        so late
        so late.

Such preordemptioned
        bitter fate.

Sounding down
        an endless hall

The ticking clock
        against the wall

The closing hands
        upon its face

If we're to make love
        we'll have to race.

Maitland Bay, NSW
1976

Laura Milligan

To Toni Savage and his
Old Wooden Printing Machine

When the great tree
Loomed from high-falling,
Her green head pitching down
Till the great body lay stillstraight,
Was she to be heard no more?
Men took her,
Piece by piece
And togethered her again,
In new bowen shape
   and from her dead body
Words came, and those printed sounds
Were stamped with loving care on
   the warp and binded weave
   of a paper made—from her sister.
Sober truth survives
Her breeze still blows
on the mind of men
and sinks such roots
As no tree, has ever sunk.

Jack Hobbs

Laura Milligan

Sun

Open ended orb
Timeless energen thing
Power beyond thought
Unharnessed might
Flaming! Hydrogen-face of God
Did you have a population problem once
and solve it.?

Diane

When you unleash the dogs of you
Onto my greenacious field
I know they are hunting.

I have seen you before
       tree tall dream,
       hair like Dane Gelt

If you are true
       then hunt me down
       but make the kill quick
I cannot live long
       in your arrowed gaze

Messages on burned Restaurant quick paper
       carry cups of red assent
Let me spill them on your Oberon-blade corsage.

Hurry White Queen,
       My Sun is setting.

Abstract

Somewhere,
    deep in the miniscule microcosms
        of unknown time,
Lost in a space within space,
a Giant of nothingness.
No sight but vibra-senses can behold
        its roaring silence.
Fillings of lustrous unknown colours,
Such primeval cold that frost melts at its maw.
Endless ice-orchid sealed in weightless jade
      that sparks with Titanic fury
      melts rainbows that liquify
      into cups of feather like ore
      drunk by basalt black figures
      who claim to have seen God.

They say, if you look through the holes in Christ's
hands you can see,
Victoria Station, only its red.

In a plane over
the Red Sea
February 1977

39

To Doug Rouse-Woodcarver

Lonely man,
What's this strange tale?
Locked in some haunted
                man free forest
You welt a wooden virgin
That was taken by a swollen stream
And this new chiselled Mary
                quick with river child
Looks her Oaken eyes on a strange Bethlehem
She had never seen before.
Villagers, seeing her in her wild beauty
Took her, and locked her in the Post Office
So no trees would fall on her.
The lonely man carved her again
                so that her Jesus child
                would not be born in a Post Office.

Laura Milligan

Summary Dawn

My sleeping children are still flying dreams
        in their goose-down heads.
The lush of the river singing morning songs
Fish watch their ceilings turn sun-white.
The grey-green pike lances upstream
Kale, like mermaids' hair
        points the water's drift.
All is morning hush
        and bird beautiful.

If only,
  I didn't have flu.

Winchelsea
1961

Jack Hobbs

Rachmaninov's 3rd Piano Concerto

We are drinking cupped Sonatas like wine,
The red glow, the cut throat of Sunset.
Like a tungsten locked Icarus
I charge my mind with heaven fermented grape
that grow to Caesar Royal Purple in my brain,
Trim my logic as I may
The tyrant Onos unbraids my thoughts
    like maidens' tresses at eve
I am wafting across mindless heavens
'Where am I,' I ask the Lotus maiden,
She says 'Singapore Air Lines—
    Economy Class'.

To A Victorian Doll in a shop window in Kensington Church Street—Priced £200

Beautiful, porcelain yester-doll,
    still wax fresh
Some little girl all ringlets
    and flounced lace
Loved you, cried on you, slept happy
    in your glass-eyed gaze.
Those long shed safe dreams
    have slipped their moorings.
That great red brick house
    spick-span polished proud
Now hard-boarded uni-rooms reeking
    curry, cabbage and cat's piss.
Polished doors lie Dulux deep,
    with red plastic handles.
So, dear home-less doll in the window
    waiting the right price
    they've turned you into a whore.

Laura Milligan

Open Heart University

Dedicated to BBC-TV Open University

We've come a long way
           said the Cigarette Scientist
as he destroyed a live rabbit
           to show the students how it worked.

He took its heart out
           plugged it into an electric pump
           that kept it beating for nearly two hours.

I know rabbits who can keep their hearts
           beating for nearly seven years

And look at the electricity they save.

London
March 1977

Laura Millgan

I thought I saw Jesus
           on a tram.
I said 'Are you Jesus?'
He said 'Yes I am'.

I thought I saw Jesus
       on a Tram.
I said 'Are you Jesus'
He said " Yes I am'.

M.1. Way of Life

Bloody, Battered, Tattered Thing
Which is body
Which is wing
What kind of bird
It's hard to say
As you lay squashed
On a motor way
But the marks in your blood
Are sharp and clear
A Dunlop 'safety' tyre
Has just been here.

Laura Milligan

I had walked out of the dead winter.
I could see a Spring child laughing through
                              the window.
Unseen fruit pulses in the arms of
                              winter trees
Young to be-bees think of honey
soon—
One less bee
One less Spring
One more Winter.

Los Angeles
June 1975

Child Songs

There is a song in man
There is a song in woman
And that is the child's song
When that song comes
There will be no words
Do not ask where they are
Just listen to the song
Listen to it—
Learn it—
It is the greatest song of all.

London
12 April 1973
0200 hours

Strange lovers may caress you
but once, long ago
you were mine for ever,
So should I reach into that past
and touch you with invisible fingers
don't move away.

Letters

I was thinking of letters,
We all have a lot in our life
A few good—a few sad
But mostly run of the mill—
I suppose that's my fault
For writing to run of the mill people.
I've never had a letter
I *really* wanted
It might come one day
But then, it will be just too late,
And that's when I don't want it.

Jack Hobbs

Timeless time and endless days
The world around us standing still
Like photographs
Of deserted shafts
Of statues left on distant hills
Two ghostly stands
In a giant's hands
We would walk together,
You and I
And the only word
From the mocking bird
Was love.

The sheer delight
Of endless light
What used to be
A barren tree
Was growing flowers overnight
And scenting it with ecstasy
A cup of coffee from your hand
Becomes the gold of Samarkand.

The swallows came and flew away
As the early dust of Autumn leaves
Were settling slow
On the afterglow
On a lasting love that could not die
When suddenly
On a tideless sea
How the glass that held us both together
Shattered and the whole damned thing went wrong.

A thousand nights
A thousand days
Are bitter pills
Time can't erase
The child we grew
Within us two
Will never know our golden days
He'll never walk
or laugh or run
Into a field
A setting sun . . . .

Laura Milligan

Catford 1933

The light creaks
    and escalates to rusty dawn
The iron stove ignites the freezing room.
Last night's dinner cast off
    popples in the embers.
My mother lives in a steaming sink.
Boiled haddock condenses on my plate
    Its body cries for the sea.
My father is shouldering his braces like a rifle,
    and brushes the crumbling surface of his suit.
The *Daily Herald* lays jaundiced on the table.
'Jimmy Maxton speaks in Hyde Park',
My father places his unemployment cards
    in his wallet–there's plenty of room for them.
In greaseproof paper, my mother wraps my
        banana sandwiches.
It's 5.40. Ten minutes to catch that
    last workman train.
Who's the last workman? Is it me? I might be famous.
My father and I walk out and are eaten by
    yellow freezing fog.
Somewhere, the Prince of Wales
    and Mrs Simpson are having morning tea in bed.
God Save the King.
But God help the rest of us.

Trust

Painful though it was,
      I cut my last winter rose for her.

She turned it inside out
      to see who the manufacturer was.

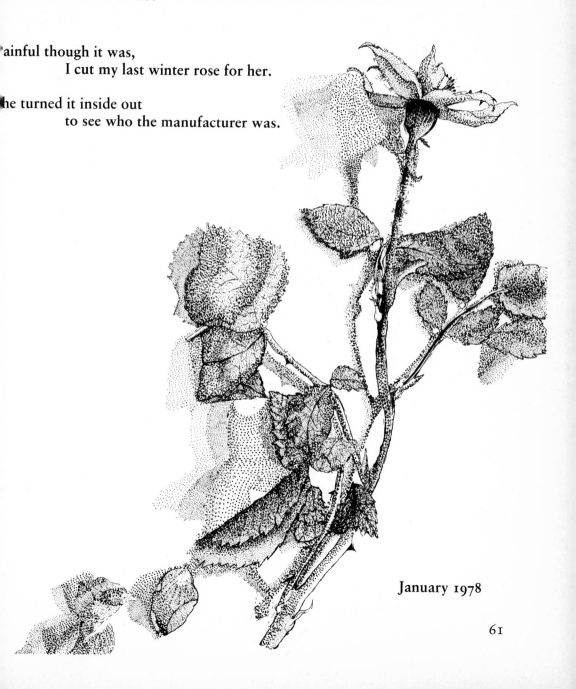

January 1978

I went to the Jazz Club.
Young over-amplified men played Saxophones
They played very fast—
Perhaps they had a bus to catch?
The drummer played very loud,
Was he deaf?
They were very accomplished musicians
The music didn't touch me
I couldn't hear the tune for the noise.
'It's not in here' said an old man.
'I'll show you where.'
He took me to an old house,
Dust lay thick on forgotten chairs.
In the corner was an embalmed piano
The old man raised the lid and pointed.
'It's in there' he said.

London
December 1974

'A' Levels

Those energy wrought children
     their limbs loaded into school desks.
In the shadows they are fed
         Algebra—Science—Syntax.

Outside, the ignorant
     are laughing and playing
     in the Sun.

Bayswater
January 1978

America I Love You

The fur bearing lady
        said to the Jeweller
'Can you fashion a rose of
        gold or silver?'
'Yes' said he
'Which is cheaper?' said she
'A real one' said he
'Real' said the lady, 'that's
        for the poor people.'

Los Angeles
1977

Laura Milligan

India! India!

As a boy
I watched India through fresh Empirical eyes.
Inside my young khaki head
I grew not knowing any other world.
My father was a great warrior
My mother was beautiful
        and never washed dishes,
        other people did that,
I was only 4, I remember
        they cleaned my shoes,
        made my bed.
'Ither ow'
'Kom Kurrow'
Yet, in time I found them gentler
        than the khaki people
They smiled in their poverty
After dark, when the khaki people
        were drunk in the mess
I could hear Minnima and
        her family praying in their godown.
In the bazaar the khaki men
        are brawling
No wonder they asked us to leave.

If a bird in a cage
    puts all heaven in a Rage.
How feels heaven when
    dies the billioneth battery hen

Floating Dandelion Seed

Wonderful wandering sky child
       seeking one piece of
              fertile soil

Alas, you don't find that
       in a railway station buffet
            so, you die.

But then, given time, a railway station
       buffet would kill us all.

My Love is Like a . . . .

If I gave her red roses
      would she?
If I gave her white roses
      in a bowl of wine
          would she?
I gave her green carnations
      made from dollar bills
          —and she did.

It was black .
It walked up a tree .
In the nest : a day old sparrow .
The black creature tore it apart .
That night
The black creature lay by the fire .
A lady stroked it .
"Nice pussy" she said .